THE LOST ECHOES

A collection of poems, musings, & short stories

SAKSHI KANORIA

BLUEROSE PUBLISHERS
India | U.K.

Copyright © Sakshi Kanoria 2024

All rights reserved by author. No part of this publication may be reproduced, stored in a retrieval system or transmitted in any form or by any means, electronic, mechanical, photocopying, recording or otherwise, without the prior permission of the author. Although every precaution has been taken to verify the accuracy of the information contained herein, the publisher assumes no responsibility for any errors or omissions. No liability is assumed for damages that may result from the use of information contained within.

BlueRose Publishers takes no responsibility for any damages, losses, or liabilities that may arise from the use or misuse of the information, products, or services provided in this publication.

For permissions requests or inquiries regarding this publication, please contact:

BLUEROSE PUBLISHERS
www.BlueRoseONE.com
info@bluerosepublishers.com
+91 8882 898 898
+4407342408967

ISBN: 978-93-6452-651-7

First Edition: July 2024

I miss you so much, baba, dadi, this one's for you!
I know you're not here, but I promise you will forever live on in my writing.

Preface

This book has been drawn from the depths of my heart and soul. It is a collection of 52 pieces, each based on true stories that dive into a spectrum of human emotions—passion, love, sadness, joy, and heartbreak. These are not just stories but reflections of lived experiences, both mine and others', that aim to capture the essence of what it means to be human.

The journey of writing this book has been extremely transformative for me. Through the process, I discovered that my emotional intensity is both a gift and a challenge. I realized that much of my trauma had been buried deep within, and it was through writing that I began to untangle these complex feelings. Writing became a form of therapy, helping me to organize my thoughts and make sense of my emotions. Each piece—whether a poem, eulogy, message, or anecdote—was written in moments of raw vulnerability. There were times when I wanted to give up, times when I wept uncontrollably, times when I laughed with abandon, and times when I felt my heart shatter. In exploring my feelings for each writing prompt, I often found myself journaling about experiences I hadn't even realized had impacted me so deeply.

This book is a testament to the healing power of storytelling. It is my sincere hope that these stories will resonate with you. Whether you are going through a difficult time, seeking a sense of connection, or simply looking for reassurance, I hope you find solace in these pages. Know that you are not alone, even if it feels that way. Each story is a beacon of empathy and understanding, offering a glimpse into the shared human experience.

May this book provide you with the fortitude to face your challenges, the sense of connection you may be longing for, and the reassurance that you are seen and heard. These pieces are my gift to you, drawn from my heart with the hope of offering comfort and companionship on your journey

The lost echoes

i.

and even though you might hate me now, i love you now and i loved you then.

ii.

i've already broken myself by breaking you.

iii.

i know i'm high maintenance, i know i have a constant need for reaffirmation, i know i need constant undivided attention,
and i know that these expectations led to our ruin.

but god i swear i love that mole on your face,
i love the sound of your voice when you're half asleep,
i love the way you keep touching your hair,
i love the way you mumble when you're uncertain and
i love how you know what i'm thinking just by the look on my face.

i have tried to write poems, quotes, stories about anything other than you. about the way i feel when i wake up. about the way i feel happy when i'm with my friends. about how in love my parents are. about how music makes me feel. about sunsets and sunrises.
but instead i always end up writing about how that one day you told me you miss me. i end up writing about how just the sound of your voice is enough to calm me down. i end up writing about how your absence makes me feel. i end up writing about missing you.

i want you and it scares me because you've torn me into a million pieces.
i need you and it terrifies me because what if you don't need me back

iv.

the scars fade, unlike the pain.

v.

you can drown out my voice yet it would call out your name,
you could shatter me into a million pieces yet they'd all come together at your command.

i don't think there's a single thing on this planet i hate more than knowing i love you with my whole heart.
i don't think i can stop myself from spiraling again. because you bring this out of me.
you bring out the best and the worst of me.

and i don't know what scares me more because you could tell me to bring you the stars and i'd attempt it but you could also tell me to jump off and i'd do that too.

vi.

memories cut like knives, especially yours.

vii.

mom you know, i finally deleted grandma from contacts.

viii.

they say i shouldn't hurt
they say it's my fault
but they only see what i show

drowning but not dying
living but not feeling
trying to reconnect with this world
accepting but not believing

ix.

in another multiverse
maybe,
we are on a call,
talking about our families,
our days,
songs we listen to.
and everything you once told me
that you never told a soul before

in another multiverse
maybe,
i am sitting with my friends,
telling them how much you care for me,
and then suddenly you call.
to tell me to eat breakfast because I forgot to eat at all.

in another multiverse
maybe,
i wouldn't see you leaving,
packing up our 3-hour calls,
the pictures where we were smiling,
every long discussion that we ever had,
and all of our *"i miss yous"*.

in another multiverse
maybe,
i am still what you want,
and you do not leave me.

x.

i know i shouldn't have to beg
for your time.
But
here i am still begging like
a cripple at a cross.

i know i can't love you
into loving me.
But
here i am praying,
hoping
you love me.
But
my hope is a plucked flower
slowly withering away.

i know you're going to
leave tomorrow.
But
at least
you're here today.

i wonder if you will stay
rise again for one more day
But
hope is like a needle
piercing my flesh
in every way

xi.

you loved her, so i walked

xii.

if i had to define what heartbreak was i'd say it was falling for you and actually believing that you loved me

if i had to define what heartbreak was i'd say it was hearing you say "i miss you" but knowing you didn't mean it

if i had to define what heartbreak was i'd say it was knowing you were slowly pulling away

if i had to define what heartbreak was i'd say it was seeing your eyes sparkle for her rather than me

if i had to define what heartbreak was i'd say it was crying on the bathroom floor because you kissed her today

if i had to define what heartbreak was i'd say it was trusting your pretty little lies

if i had to define what heartbreak was i'd say it was knowing you don't love me anymore

if i had to define what heartbreak was i'd say it was us

if i had to define what heartbreak was i'd say it was you

xiii.

you don't love me anymore.

maybe you don't

but why do your eyes still constantly find me in a crowded room?
why am i still the first one to know things about you?
why do you still hug me like there's no one else for you?
why do you still look at me like i shattered your whole existence when i left?
why do you still know exactly what i want when i want it?
why do you still call out for me like it's tearing you apart inside?
why do you sneak glances at me like there's no one else you'd rather look at?
why do still hold me like you're afraid i'll let go again?
why do you brush past me like you want me to ask you to stay?

xiv.

a system allowing unequal power
distribution,
leading to the detriment of women.
bringing across the illusion,
that everyone has the choice
or decision.

the father, the son
these men have authority.
unjust rules and norms made
out of their insecurity,
this system is
further escalating the gap
in our society.

the women of our nation
suffocation,
suppression,
oppression,
the liberation of our forefathers,
gave no rise to our mothers.
has this system allowed equality?

xv.

you were my homeland but now you've sent me past enemy lines and become the war zone

you were my calm but now you're the storm

you were my hearth but now you're the fire

you were my happiness but now you're the biggest blue

you were my crutch but now you're the injury

you were a part of me but now you're just the void

you were the medicine but now you're the bruise

you were the song that lulled me to sleep but now you're the voice that keeps me awake

you were my comfort but now you're the weight on my chest that i can't get rid of

you were the air i used to breathe but now you just suffocate me

and somehow somewhere along the way it became you vs me not us vs the world

xvi.

i swear nothing could do you justice. you moved mountains for us. i remember how even when you were on bedrest, your eyes were wandering about our home, checking on all of us. how one cry of pain and you'd leave no stone unturned trying to help me relieve it. how in spite of your being in immense agony you always had a smile on. how your hug could solve any problem in the world. and how despite you not understanding my problems you always solved them.

you live on in infinite people and things; in all nine of us, in every fruit i eat, in those tuberoses that fall every winter, in the paan masala that tau eats every day, in the 70's hindi songs that i promise i'll sing to my children too, in that tv show we used to watch together, in my urge to be nice to everyone i meet, in every person you've met, in every birthday, and in every papad that we ever make.

you've taught me to love everyone with all my heart, to be strong in the face of adversity, and to do the one thing i love most: cook. but above everything you've taught me that i should be kind to everyone i meet and to do things for people not because of who they are or what they do in return but because of the person you've made me.

from following our daily traditions to fighting with me on everything. from cutting fruits and feeding them to me in my mouth to saving me from mom's wrath. you've indulged me so much. thank you for your love and encouragement because that's the only thing keeping me going. thank you for making me believe in myself and my worth. thank you for getting me anything i asked for because i could've told you to bring me the stars and you would have. thank you for looking at me with so much love. thank you for always taking my side. thank you for bringing us all together and thank you mostly for making me the person i am today.

The lost echoes

i still don't know how i'm supposed to live a whole life without you but i'll pick up the pieces and do it because that's what you've taught me. i love you so much. see you on the other side of the universe.

xvii.

you were a planet and i was just a satellite.

you were the sun and i was just one of the many planets revolving around and depending on it.

but you know you are the dying sun

and with you,

all of us too are slowly
        w i t h e r i n g
                                    away.

xviii.

how can you forgive someone you thought did the unforgivable, even if that is the only thing that can give you peace?

xix.

ruin me, ruin everything and god knows i'll let you do it.

xx.

"why isn't she leaving him"
always my thought
never did i realize it might be his fault
condemned not the abuser always the abused
now i finally understand
----
take a moment to
acknowledge
the victim's plight
don't criticize
this psychological cell
"leave him"
so easy to say
her screams
you don't hear
her self-worth
stripped away
erase the agent
the biggest mistake
all the guilt she felt
it's hard to stop
limits he pushed
new each time
her sigh of relief
"he's not home"
fear, trauma
only things constant
from his fists
scars form
yet from her inaction
blame is born

xxi.

2020 was the most life-changing, heart-shattering, and informative year of my small life; especially that one day.

about 8 billion people experienced that day but no one, not a single person was as empty as i was. i think for a few days i was just a basket full of memories of you. the last time you saw me. the last time i made you roti and sabzi. the last time i fed you from my hands. the last time you laughed. the last time you said "i love you." the last time you kissed me. the last time i saw pride in your eyes.
even now sometimes this basket of memories overflows while other times it's empty.

i have such vivid memories of that day. but sometimes all i remember is those mosquitoes. those mosquitoes surrounding your body. all i remember is that box in the middle of our beautiful but now tainted house. that box that was there to keep your body cold. the box we had to put you in to keep those mosquitoes and that foul smell away. that ice box that really shouldn't have been there. but all i wanted to do at that moment was to run away from home, from that box, from our family. i just wanted to go back and wait for your call to hear your soothing voice. the only voice that could bring me back down, the voice that could calm all of us. i still remember dad had to drag me down from my room to look at you and there you were in that godforsaken box looking as beautiful as the first memory i have of you.

on my tombstone, my death year should be written as 2020 as the only part of me that was still alive, died along with you on that dreadful day.

xxii.

they say that 70% of our planet is water.
water— essential for our way of life.
without it our existence would disintegrate.
it has the power to cause the whole world to fall apart,

and
just like water takes most of our earth,
i say 70% of me is you.

you, with the power to destroy my existence or to be the reason i'm alive.

xxiii.

i used to look for you in the lyrics that once made me cry silent tears till my pillow was wet and my brain was numb
i used to look for you in the thoughts that once made me slit my wrists till i bled out on the bathroom floor and cried out for help
i used to look for you in the nightmares that i once begged to be woken up from, nightmares that made me shake and scream till my throat dried up
i used to look for you in the prayers that god never answered, in the prayers that made me completely lose my faith on him
i used to look for you in the days when i wished that i never woke up
i used to look for you in the dreams that broke and shattered into so many pieces that the shards still pierce me

but as i stared at the tainted shards, the reflection wasn't of me, but of you
for i was broken and you broke me
you took so much of me that when you left i was no longer me i was parts of you
every time i wanted to save myself i used to find you and the sliver of hope that you would be there was what destroyed me

> *yet i continued looking for you not knowing that i didn't need you to save me but you were the one i needed to be saved from.*

xxiv.

the intimacy of eating a big, messy burger in front of them

the intimacy of sitting in complete silence with them for hours without a hint of awkwardness

the intimacy of reading a book and annotating it for them

the intimacy of "i love you more than i could ever love anyone"

the intimacy of a tight hug

the intimacy of being able to cry in front of them

the intimacy of "can you check if there's something in my eyes?"

the intimacy of "when i need a break all i need is you"

the intimacy of knowing the other person's starbucks order

the intimacy of sleeping next to each other

the intimacy of unknowingly ending up in front of their house after driving for hours on end

the intimacy of seeing their pet grow up

the intimacy of knowing each other's families

the intimacy of wearing their jacket to sleep

the intimacy of knowing their smell

the intimacy of recognising the sound of their footsteps

the intimacy of finding them waiting on the couch for you to get home

the intimacy of waking up with a blanket over you when you slept without one

the intimacy of cooking together

the intimacy of holding someone's hand when they take their last breath

the intimacy of sharing songs

the intimacy of "i made you a playlist"

the intimacy of fighting

the intimacy of acceptance and gratitude.

xxv.

"meri darling toh hamesha hi sundar lagti hai."
13 years, and every day i heard these words.
13 years, and days for me to stop believing them.
why do these words… suddenly feel so hollow…
13 years and NOW is when your darling needs to be called pretty.
who do i look for now?

even if you're gone i know we'll never be apart
13 years, lying on your chest just hearing the beats of your heart
seeing how they merge into mine,
13 years, but i still can't tell myself that i'm fine
you gave me the strength to believe it,
where do i find it now?

7 billion people in the world
and death had to stop at your feet
you were sheer perfection, not even diamonds could compete
and all i believe is i'm not worthy
how can i hate myself when it's your heart that's beating in mine?

xxvi.

everyday a cycle of drowning,
being pulled under the waves,
except the ocean was not filled with water but my hopelessness like
i was drowning but without death's *release.*

xxvii.

how do i compete with someone who seems to be your other half?
how do i compete with someone who seems to always make you laugh?
at the end of a hard day it's only her that makes you smile.
what would i be if i tried to take that away?

xxviii.

it's not that i don't love you, it's that day when i woke up in the middle of the night because of my sister's screaming and crying in the middle of her house. it's how the walls shook, the roof echoed her screams, all portraying her agony. my heart cracked a little that day.

it's not that i don't love you it's that day she realized that they were not the end even though he was for her in one way. it's the way she booked her flights back home cause she couldn't handle being alone; this was coming from a girl who loved her independence but at that point just wanted her mother's embrace, her father's presence, and her sisters' 'i told you so.'

it's not that i don't love you it's the look on her face when she saw him with another girl. it's the sobbing, the howling, the hurt. it's how she didn't eat for weeks and drowned herself in her workouts and coffee breaks; constantly surviving but not living. my heart cried with her.

it's not that i don't love you it's just that i don't want to leave this surreal world for the harsh reality this word comes with. and if i could feel that much pain through her i don't want to know what would happen if you left.

xxix.

i wear my jeans differently now because she told me that they're supposed to be worn that way. i eat kimbap every time i'm at a korean restaurant because it reminds me of him. i add bay leaves to my arrabbiata sauce because she once told me it adds taste to it. i eat mangoes every summer after every hard day because he once said "mangoes make everything better." i can't listen to jeremy zucker songs without thinking of him and there are certain songs i don't listen to because we used to listen to them together. i drink my coffee with more sugar just so he would like it if he wanted a sip. i buy extra chocolates whenever i buy them just so i would have some if she wanted them. i keep an extra hundred in my wallet because he once said "keep a hundred rupee note just so i know you're safe." i can never hear the word 'cruise' without laughing and thinking of them. and i can't think of the word 'moti' without remembering my name on his phone.

i think i'm a little bit of him and a little bit of her and a little bit of everyone i meet. some people remain a part of you even when they leave, maybe as a lesson, maybe as a story worth telling, or maybe as a gift.

xxx.

will i ever be the one?
hatred fails me
it's never failed me before
but how can i hate her when she's the only one making you smile?

i tried a million times
yellow, sunshine in human form
i tried so desperately to be her
she was your kryptonite
a daisy, beautiful, humble, and kind
i really did try to be her
the silence now deafening
it took over
your eyes were watering,
hopelessness suddenly visible on your face
i tried to smile, focusing on the memory of what was once you and me
i tried a million times
will i ever be enough?

now,
i'm done trying
blue, the bluest of blues
it's the color i've embodied
the exact opposite of her
i'm never gonna be her
a hyacinth, jealous, sad, and alone
i'm sorry a sorry won't ever be enough
it won't ever be enough for making me feel like i wasn't enough
i tried a million times

**now,
i'm done trying.**

xxxi.

sinking, that's what it feels like
i'm drowning and you didn't even notice
i'm torn in half, water's seeping through
slowly filling till this body can't tell itself apart
the parts of me, now, so far apart, carried away
slowly
s
  i
    n
      k
        i
          n
            g

xxxii.

i was angry when you died.
the anger faded,
wishing you were here never did.

xxxiii.

sometimes, the heartache feels like home, familiar and comforting in its own way.
but then there are days, it's a prison i can't escape.

xxxiv.

atlas, how long before we both get to see the sun again?

xxxv.

you're an ocean
95% not even partially discovered
i'm here left to wonder how much more we could be

you're an ocean
your shallow waters, they leave me vulnerable to the suns deathly gaze
but your depths, they might suffocate me but i've never been one to heed the warnings

xxxvi.

but a bouquet of warm hugs turned to flowers of a funeral when i saw her face.

xxxvii.

i still hear his silvery voice even though it didn't sound the same when i was with him in that room.

i still see his old, handsome face even though it wasn't the same in the car; it was a color between blue and green.

i still feel his rough, wrinkly hands; they used to be warm, but they were as cold as ice that day.

I still smell his soft floral trail from his perfume and try to forget the foul smell that gathered mosquitoes on his body.

xxxviii.

i don't want to break, i can't.
but
the way you look at me is enough to shatter me into pieces that i don't think you could pick up

xxxix.

but it's easier to blame someone you don't love and someone who's not dead.

xxxx.

tomorrow, i could stop feeling resentful. tomorrow, i could just forgive.
but
tomorrow is not today, and that's how it is.

xxxxi.

so, that's what i did, i broke you before you could break me.

xxxxii.

and while i'm trying to tape myself together i wish i could tape us back together too.

xxxxiii.

you taught me how to love,
but never how to stop.
now i'm lost,
in a sea of broken hearts

xxxxiv.

every song i hear, reminds me of you,
a melody of memories, i can't forget.

xxxxv.

i've tried to hate you,
to erase you from my mind,
to scrub you from my body
but love doesn't work that way,
it lingers,
it stays.

xxxxvi.

i waited for an answer, but all i got was silence.

xxxxvii.

"to every you i'll never be with"
i'll never get to see you grow up with me
side my side, you and me against the world
maybe polar opposites, maybe exactly the same
we never got to figure that out
the daughter, the sister, the twin
you'll always be in my heart

for most of my life i never knew you existed
although i felt your void
maybe you would've been the biggest part of me
maybe you still are
i'm sorry i don't remember you
but i'll always miss you
maybe you're here maybe you're with baba dadi
i hope wherever you are you're happy

i make a promise to you since you couldn't live your life i promise to live ours to the fullest

here's to you, the girl who looked exactly like me but the girl i could never be with

xxxxviii.

we built our dreams on shattered hopes,
we built our love on broken hearts,
we built our trust on whispered lies,
we built us on fragile starts.

even as the walls crumbled,
we built.

xxxxix.

the "i love you" that stays locked in our throats,
the "i'm sorry" that remains unuttered,
the "i miss you" that echoes in our hearts but never reaches their ears.

are the silent shadows that linger in the spaces between us, a reminder of the words we never dared to speak.

The lost echoes

xxxxx.

your absence– a presence,
a void that fills every room.

xxxxxi.

in the quiet of the night,
in the whispers of the wind,
in the shadows of the past,
in the tears that never end.
i love you *still*

Acknowledgement

Firstly, I want to acknowledge myself—for facing life's challenges and finding the strength to write this book

To all my heartbreaks (you know who you are), you are the reason this book exists. Your impact on my life provided the inspiration and the words for these poems. Thank you for being a part of my story, even if it was painful.

A heartfelt thank you to Diya Bubber for her incredible artistry in creating the book's front and back cover. Your talent has brought my words to life in the most beautiful way.

To my family, thank you for your unwavering support and for always pushing me to follow my dreams. Your encouragement has been my foundation and my strength.

To my friends, thank you for always being there. Your love and support mean the world to me, and I couldn't have done this without you. You have been my constant source of joy and encouragement.

Smita Aunty, Ms Vandana, and Mr. Robertson, your guidance and assistance in editing have been invaluable. Thank you for your unwavering and consistent support and for helping me refine my work.

I also want to acknowledge anyone I may have missed, whose contributions, whether big or small, have played a part in this journey. Your support, even in the smallest ways, has not gone unnoticed.

Lastly, I want to extend my gratitude to every reader who has picked up this book. Your interest and engagement with my work is the ultimate reward. I hope these poems resonate with you and offer solace, connection, and understanding.

With deepest gratitude,

Sakshi Kanoria

Author's Note

In an effort to contribute to environmental conservation, this book is available in a digital format as well. By choosing to digitize my work, I aim to reduce the demand for paper and the subsequent deforestation that results from it. Every year, 4.1 million hectares of forest are cut down to satisfy the global need for paper.

I encourage you to share this book with your loved ones. Not only can we help someone in their time of need, but we can also make a positive impact on the environment. Together, we can create a ripple effect of both emotional support and ecological preservation.

www.ingramcontent.com/pod-product-compliance
Lightning Source LLC
LaVergne TN
LVHW061602070526
838199LV00077B/7145